MW00720532

Reflections Thru My Windshield

Part 2

Dave Madill

Best wishes Sue

Dave Madill

Bookworm.

July 05/08

Reflections Thru My Windshield
Part 2
Copyright © 2007 by David R. Madill

A **Write Up The Road** Book

For more information contact:
Write Up The Road Publishing
P.O. Box 69
Kenton, TN 38233
(800) 292-8072
www.writeuptheroad.com

Reflections Thru My Windshield   Part 2
Madill, David R.
ISBN: 09766872-9-1

Cover design by Tim Brady
Printed in the United States of America

Reflections

Reflected through my windshield, this old world I see

Sometimes smeared with dust or bugs; it's there in front of me

From the glaciers of Alaska to the sands of Mexico,

From east coast to the west coast as down the roads I go.

The mountains in their splendor, the wild and rocky shore

The plains with all their bounty, no man could ask for more.

The cities with their clamor, their bustle and their pain

Ever changing, ever growing as I pass by again.

The homeless as they wander, the lawyer with his brief

The farmer with a field of grain and a proud old Indian Chief;

So many different stories waiting to be told,

Reflected through my windshield as I pass along the road.

Table of Contents

On the Road   1
The Cabin   2
Solitude   3
Jim   4-5
The Writer   6
Spirit   7
Lady Driver   8
Death and Life   9
A Simple Church   10
Old Memories   11
Old Glory   12
A Child's Eyes   13
Nameless Ones   14
Greasy Grass   15
Dance with Me   16
I Will Stand   17
The Beach   18
Quiet Voices   19
The Seawall   20
The Highway   21
The Knight   22-23
The Ride   24-25
Perception   26
Hang Glide   27
Connected   28
Shared Dream   29
Echoes   30
Middle of Nowhere   31
Winter Dispatch   32
Hurry Up and Wait   33
Winter Solitude   34
Secrets out of time   35
Drums and Bugles   36
Space Travelers   37
Beside You   38
Hold On   39
Life's Load   40
The Lady of the Lake   41
Again The Horsemen Ride   42
The Game   43
The Compromise   44
Lonely Sounds   45
There Stands a Glass   46

The Sentry	47
The Lady and Her Legacy	48
Apart	49
Did You	50
Cold City	51
I Go On	52
The Moonbeam	53
Big Rig Thunder	54
Darkness	55
Another Day	56
Wanderers	57
Fallen Star	58
She	59
Behind the Man	60
Silent Wonder	61
I Held His Hand	62
Sinner Man	63
Fire on the Mountain	64
Last Gunfighter	65
Daydreams	66
A Voice	67
The Old Man	68
The Old Man Part 2	69
Her Eyes	70
Autumn Pause	71
Two Lovers	72
Three Prayers	73
Dragon Tales	74
Errant Knight	75
What will you remember	76
The Light	77
The Waitress	78
Greasy Grass Revisited	79
Tired Eyes	80
The Forgotten	81
Silence	82
A Flower	83
Gentle Passage	84
Eternal Drive	85
Broken Heart	86
Listen	87
Our Lady	88
She Cries	89
Gentle Memories	90
Empty Arms	91

vi

Summer Storm   92
Dreams and Wishes   93
A Woman's Power   94
Afterglow   95
Time will Tell   96
Somebody's Knocking   97
The Meadow   98
A Child's Cry   99
Helping Hand   100
Dark City Night   101
Still Working   102
A Picture   103
The Lady Cries   104
A Common Soldier   105
Our Trail   106
Endless Sky   107
An Old Truck   108
A Simple Life   109
Let's Stop   110
Atlantic Shore   111
Winding Road   112
My Luck   113
Sit with Me   114
A Simple Hand   115
A Trucker's Prayer   116
Children   117
The Old Truck   118

On the Road

I travel down the highway and I do the best I can,

Not a knight in shining armor, just a diesel-driving man.

When there is an accident, we're usually at the scene,

Helping pull the people from their broken-up machines.

When you break down on the highway,
we're the ones you flag down,

We will help to change a tire or drive you into town.

When you merge on the highway, we try to let you in

We will also call the troopers if you had too much gin.

Out there on the highways, pulling our heavy loads,

We see so many things as we travel down the roads.

All we ask is some respect, and maybe a little smile,

As we pull all the things you need across these lonely miles.

Give us just some room to breathe, in our shiny steeds of steel,

That could be your son or daughter that sits behind the wheel.

The Cabin

A little cabin in the pines where snow is gently falling

Somewhere in the gathering dusk I hear a wild wolf calling

The doors are locked and the fire burns bright

Cuddled on a bearskin rug I hold my lover tight

Firelight dances across our skin and we care not for the weather

To the rhythm of the wild our bodies come together.

Solitude

I slip across the water, silence all around

Paddle dipping slowly, I hardly make a sound

Reflected in the water I see the quiet hills;

A light mist clouds the reflection; the lake is dark and still.

Then a lonely, lovely sound; the calling of a loon

Its mate calls back in answer, all nature is in tune.

My canoe moves quietly as darkness falls around,

Slowly I pull to the shore and stand on solid ground.

A campfire is my beacon, a gentle kind of light,

Solitude is my companion in the stillness of the night.

Jim

He walked into the café, on his face a quiet smile;

Only if you knew him, could you see the lonely miles.

Jessie asked about his family and he said that they were fine.

Me, I never said a word, but I knew that he was lying.

You see, Jim was my brother, and I knew about his life,

I knew all his troubles with his damned cheating wife.

Jim sat down at our table, and we talked about our loads,

I warned him about the canyon and the ice upon the roads.

We talked for about an hour; then we got up to leave,

Jim gave Jess and me a big old hug; whispered,

"Promise not to grieve."

We watched his taillights disappear that cold and rainy night,

I felt a chill come over me as he went out of sight.

I guess Jess felt it too, 'cause I heard her give a little moan.

I turned, and she was crying; she said, "Jim is going home."

I knew I could not catch him; my truck was way too slow,

We stood there in the parking lot as the rain turned into snow.

We delivered in the morning; that's when I called in,

They told me then about the wreck,

and how we lost my brother Jim.

They blamed the wreck upon the road, all that ice and snow,

Me, I say it was suicide; and I'm the only one who knows.

The Writer

Just slightly out of step with time, in a world that does not care

The tortured pathways of his mind, somehow he wanders there;

Alone upon his journeys, thru the future and the past,

Castles he builds on shifting sands and dreams that do not last.

Yet with his written word, somehow he takes us there.

His tales of fact, or fiction; even his dreams we share.

He takes us to the stars or across a desert bare,

As we read between the lines, we are transported there.

The magic of the printed word from the writer's busy hand,

Stronger than a sword of steel, is heard throughout the land.

Spirit

I have wandered through eternity, my spirit has run free.

For a thousand years or so I was a redwood tree...

Then I was an eagle, soaring across the sky,

Reading currents in the air; soaring there on high.

As a cougar I was predator, as a mouse I was prey

Always though, I did my best each and every day.

I've been a King, I've been a slave, my body bought and sold,

A sailor on the seven seas, my story still untold.

Someday I'll fly a starship across the universe so wide,

Who can tell what I will be, there on the other side.

I know my spirit will live on, wherever I may be,

Perhaps I'll take a little rest, and again I'll be a tree...

Lady Driver

She drives along the Interstate in her steed of glass and steel,

She's as good as any driver that sits behind the wheel.

She's a wife and she's a mother, she's a lover, she's a friend

She is out here on that highway that never seems to end.

Like every other driver, she gripes about the pay

But she has special problems that she faces every day.

The shippers and receivers treat her different than a man,

Still she tries to carry on and do the best she can.

Male drivers on the highway sometimes cause her strife

Yet still she carries on; it's part of her way of life.

Does she search for something special,

or is she searching for someone,

Has she become addicted to the diesel's throaty hum?

The highway has a lonely call, and it's heard far and near

Now it has a different voice and it sings out load and clear.

She is out there on that highway in her steed of glass and steel,

The equal to any man when she's behind the wheel.

Death and Life

Alone out on the highway, I wander in my mind

I wander back in memory to other places, other times.

Huddled around a campfire, I hear a wild wolf howl

I shiver in my cloak of skins; death is on the prowl.

Another campfire, another time, sword and armor by my side

I hear the sound of a charging horse; death takes a nighttime ride.

Next a dark and moonless night, I see by cockpit lights

A bomber sows its deadly seeds; death rides the sky tonight.

Then I see him standing there, dressed in a robe of white,

He reaches out to take my hand and leads me toward the light.

If you will just believe, my son, then you need never die;

I give the gift of eternal life to those that really try.

You need never fear, my son, just place your hand in mine,

We will dwell together until the end of time.

A Simple Church

Just a simple country church where common people pray,

Nestled there among the pines, drab in the light of day

They gather every Sunday when that old bell rings,

Common folk from all around, come to kneel and pray and sing.

There are no stained glass windows, no spires to the sky

Just a place to worship and to say goodbye to those who die.

A simple place of worship, a place of peace and hope

Where people come together to help each other cope.

A simple church, within the pines, filled with peace and love

A place where common people seek God's eternal love.

Old Memories

I have walked the dusty gravel roads and heard the westbound train

Even though those days are gone, in my mind I walk again

Splash in the swimming hole; in the water, deep and clear

Visit that old farmhouse and see the ones I held so dear.

Gather 'round the kitchen table at the ending of the day

Visit that old country church, kneel again and pray.

Wander through the forest where we tapped the maple trees

Stand beside a field of grain bending in the gentle breeze.

Visit that one-room schoolhouse and see the schoolyard

where we did play,

There I learned the lessons that are with me still today.

Love of God and country and the need to speak the truth,

The many things I cherish, I learned there as a youth.

Gentle summer evenings, the sound of a Whippoorwill

Gathered around the kitchen stove, as winter winds blew chill

Many years have come and gone, these times are in the past

Although they may be over, my memories will last.

Old Glory

I've been trod on and I've been burned

I've been cursed and I've been spurned

Many things I've stood for have been thrown back in my face

In the search for truth and justice others have tried to take my place

Governments have come and gone, systems arose and fell

Yet if you choose to listen, there's a story I would tell:

My blue stands for the skies and the seas that wash my shore

My red is blood that has been shed; pray there be no more

My white stands for purity of word, thought and deed

My stripes are the colonies where liberty was but a seed

My stars are many states that we have joined as one

We will all stand together; we will not hide or run.

I have flown on foreign shores and across the oceans deep

Liberty and justice are promises I will keep

I will not bow to tyrants and I will not hide my face

When the battles are all over, I will stand in my rightful place.

A Child's Eyes

I have walked foreign shores and crossed the mountains high

Soared aloft on silent wings and wheeled across the sky

I've fished our mighty rivers and seen Grizzlies in the wild;

Nothing beats the wonder I see in the eyes of a child.

A child sees a ray of sunshine, or a single drop of rain,

They see them as a marvel that may never come again.

We in all our wisdom look through jaded eyes

We do not see the beauty or the wonder of the skies.

Children in their innocence see things we do not see;

The softness of a snowflake or the beauty of a tree

The marvel of a sunset or a single drop of rain.

Could we look through their eyes and see these things again;

If we saw through a child's eyes, would there still be war and strife

Or would we see the beauty that surrounds us in this life?

Could we do away with hardship, and do away with all the lies,

Could we live in truth and beauty, looking through a child's eyes?

Nameless Ones

Who are these nameless ones that sit behind the wheel

Knights in faded denim in their steeds of glass and steel

Do they have a lover waiting, or perhaps a broken home

Does someone join them in their dreams or do they cry alone?

Do they pause to see a sunset or walk in gently falling rain,

Do they smile in happiness or cry aloud in pain?

So many nameless drivers, with their stories still untold

The thunder of their engines still echoes down the road.

Greasy Grass

I walk along the Greasy Grass; feel the prairie winds grow chill

Then I hear the sounds of battle from just below the hill,

The stench of the black powder, the copper smell of blood

Seems to come from all around me, strikes me like a flood

Battle all around me, I hear the wounded cry

In the midst of this great battle, was I the one that died?

Did I ride with Sitting Bull or stand with Yellow Hair

Was I but a lowly horse that took his last breath there.

What is it in this haunted place, that reaches for my soul,

Could I be somehow connected to this battle long ago?

Do those that gave their lives, still have something to give

Could it be a warning, to those of us who live

Again I feel the prairie wind, which whispers to my mind

Memories of long ago, like echoes out of time.

Dance with Me

Dance with me, my little one, while the fiddles play

Put your arms around me, let me feel your body sway

Let me look into your eyes, while I hold you in my arms

You know I am a prisoner, captured by your charms

Let me kiss you tenderly, as they turn the lights down low

Dance with me, my darling, till it is time to go.

Let me hold you in my arms, and feel the years slip away

Waltz with me across the floor, back to a younger day.

Dance with me, my darling, listen to the music play

Let me hold you in my arms forever and a day.

I Will Stand

I will stand and fight for country, God and home

For liberty, and freedom; and I will not stand alone.

Tempered by a Mother's love, raised by my Father's hand

Peace and freedom my birthright in this, the best of lands.

My forefathers fought for freedom in this and foreign lands,

Now the sword is passed to me, now I will make my stand.

Like other men before me, my blood I give if I must,

I will fight for freedom, and I know my cause is just.

I fight because I have to, as men must not live in fear

For those that went before me, I shed a silent tear

I will stand and fight for country, God and home

For liberty, and freedom; and I will not be alone.

The Beach

She walks along a quiet beach, a memory by her side

Sits upon a storm-tossed log, watches the ebbing tide

The receding waters uncover rocks and sand

So much like her very life, he's water; she's the land

The rocks are the many fears she faces every day

They seem to grow much larger whenever he's away.

The little wavelets chuckle as they slowly slip away

They seem to say, he will be back once again to play;

She whispers a quiet prayer, "Lord, keep him safe from harm,

Bring him back home to me, to nestle in my arms."

Then she sheds a silent tear and goes along her way

Just another trucker's wife, just another day.

Quiet Voices

I wandered through the forest; stopped, and listened to the trees

Heard the gentle murmur as they swayed there in the breeze

The quiet babble of the brook, which flows across the stones

So like a lover's whisper calling out, "Come Home."

The quiet voices of the birds as they call to one another

Squirrels playing in the tree, playing tag with each other

Nature gently calls to me and soothes me as I stand

A simple child of nature touched by Mother Nature's hand.

The Seawall

I walked along the seawall by the ocean way out west

Waves were pounding on the shore but the seawall stood the test

A storm upon the ocean; waves march toward the land

Crash upon the beaches, and ebb back across the sand.

Then the storm is over and gentle breezes blow

Little wavelets caress the land, and gentle currents flow

The interaction of sea and land reminds me so much of life

The many trials and troubles between a husband and a wife

Love can be a seawall, bound with trust and respect

Anchored down with common sense, it can pass any test

Walk along life's storm beaches together, hand in hand

Then when the gentle breezes blow, walk gently in the sand.

The Highway

This highway reaches out to me, and touches my very soul

This mistress of my destiny, tells me to let it roll

She tells of greener pastures as I thunder through the night;

Always over another hill, just to the left or right,

What is this hold she has on me, why do I answer to her song

She is a taker; not a giver, and this road, it is so long,

Was I born to wander always, to look over that next hill

To listen to coyotes sing and hear the lonely whippoorwill

The call of an air horn, the way the tires cry

The thunder of a diesel as it goes sailing by

Why do I heed this call, listen to her lonely song

This cold and heartless mistress keeps me ever moving on.

The Knight

She walked out to her driveway, that cold December night

Stopped and wished upon a star; wishing for a knight

A man on a white stallion to carry her away,

One to keep her safe from harm forever and a day.

Of course, nothing happened; there was no flash of light

Slowly she climbed into her car, as she had to work tonight

Just three miles down the highway, right on the edge of town

She had to be there on time, so she pressed the pedal down.

Everything was going fine until she hit the ice,

She felt the car start to slide, then turn around twice,

Backwards then, into the ditch; it slowly came to rest

Settled into the snow bank, like a bird upon a nest.

Then a man was by her door, as she began to shake

She never saw his big rig stop, never heard him brake.

Gently he helped her from the car; asked if she was all right,

Asked where she was going on that cold December night.

She told him of the diner, and he offered her a ride

He helped her up into his truck and she settled down inside.

He drove her to the diner, and sent a tow truck for her car,

Then as he sat and talked to her, she thought about that star

Was this a Knight in faded Levis, with a steed of glass and steel?

How very gentle he had been, but so sure behind the wheel.

The Knight
Page 2

That was seven years ago, and he'll be home sometime today,

She has so much to tell him: Their second child is on the way.

They still laugh about the way they met,

the night she ditched the car.

She sometimes has a special smile, when she gazes on a star.

The Ride

He was half-way down that mountain pass,

and his heart was in his mouth

His tractor, it was pointed west; but the trailer pointed south.

The trailer hit the guardrail, and he felt the tractor sway,

He slammed his hand down on the spike - then he began to pray

He was grabbing for the shifter when the trailer hit some dirt,

Snapped straight in behind him, without anything being hurt.

He dropped her down a pair of gears,

and heard that old Jake brake howl,

It sounded like a jungle cat out upon the prowl.

When he hit the level ground, he pulled off of the road,

Then got out and walked around, checked his tires and his load.

Later, at the diner, he told us about his ride

He was 'quite a little driver,' he pointed out with pride.

I sat and listened quietly, and then I had my say,

"What makes you think you were alone, upon the hill today?

You told us you said a prayer to keep it on the road,

Perhaps it was an Angel's wing that saved you and your load."

The diner got real quiet; then he replied, "You're right.

I guess I have Someone to thank, when I lie down tonight."

As we travel down the highway, sometimes we are not alone,

Sometimes Angels sit beside us, to help us make it home.

Perception

We struggle from our time of birth to walk, to talk, to cry,

Always reaching forward until the day we die

Yet there is wonder in a child's eyes, as he perceives a tree

As he sees an eagle fly, soaring wild and free

We must take time in our lives to revisit the days of our youth,

Perhaps if we could stand and stare, we might perceive the truth.

Hang Glide

High above the ground below, on silent wings I fly

I bank and turn; then soar aloft, reach out and touch the sky

Too soon the land reaches out for me, and I return to earth

Grounded now by gravity, grounded by my birth.

Still I have soared with eagles, and swept across the sky

That freedom stays within me until the day I die.

Connected

Somewhere in the dark of night a newborn child cries

Somewhere in a lonely bed another old man dies

The child is facing forward, the future is his prize

The old man he looks backward, the past is in his eyes

Yet they are joined together in the brotherhood of man

Both must work together to be all that they can.

The child must look behind him and learn from our mistakes

The old men must look forward to teach youth what it takes.

One is born and one dies, and they will not meet each other,

Yet connected by the sands of time they will work together.

Shared Dream

You slipped into my dream tonight like smoke from a candle flame

You smiled and kissed me gently, and I heard you say my name

Lost in the ecstasy, I held you in my arms

I surrendered to the passion, a prisoner of your charms.

Then in a moment you were gone, like a thief into the night

You were not there when I awoke to see the morning light

Your scent upon my pillow, a hint of perfume in the air

Was I only dreaming or were you really there?

Darling, join me in my dream beneath the pale moonlight

Together in a dream we share, we will love throughout the night.

Echoes

The quiet stillness of the night is harshly ripped asunder

A big rig moves on down the road

with a sound like rolling thunder

Clearance lights and headlight beams

stab through the gloom of night

Chrome and steel glow softly in the flicker of moonlight

Then in a moment they are gone, taillights a distant glow

The echo of their passing stirs the gently swirling snow.

Middle of Nowhere

In the middle of nowhere, earth seems to touch the sky

Time seems to hold its breath, gives a gentle sigh

Time has no meaning here, and silence is a sound

Clouds pause in wonder, reach and touch the ground

Man is an intruder here, yet there is room to live

The gentle fertile Mother Earth has so much to give

How we accept this challenge, with humor and with tears

Shows others our courage, and helps us through the years.

Winter Dispatch

Snow drifts across the highway; and I drop down another gear,

The road looks like polished glass and I find it hard to steer.

There is no need to hurry, trucks shuffle into line

Dispatch sees it differently; they want me there on time.

Still, out on this highway, I'll have the final say

I am the one who'll choose to drive, or to wait another day.

Safety is my watchword; no load is worth my life

I have too much to live for, my children and my wife.

Still at times I push the edge; it's the only life I know

Steadily I push on, through a night of ice and snow.

Hurry Up and Wait

Seems no matter where I go, it's hurry up and wait:

Got to have you there on time; then sat outside the gate.

Throw the logbook out the window and *get in there on time*

I get in at four o'clock - then hit the dock at nine.

Go over to the shipper and *be there at ten o'clock*

Eleven hours later I pull out from the dock.

No matter what the conditions, no matter what the road

Every load is just in time; they are all waiting for my load.

Winter Solitude

Stars sparkle in the heavens and a full moon sheds its glow,

Fields glisten hard as diamond beneath a covering of snow.

A rabbit in his coat of white hides from the bright moonlight

A Snowy Owl on silent wings searches the northern night.

Birch and Aspen glisten in the ghostly pale moonlight

Pine trees stand like sentinels in their heavy coats of white.

I pause in my travels, and in wonderment I stand,

Surrounded by the silence of a winter wonderland.

Secrets out of time

Away up north of sixty, there's a land of ice and snow

There stand lofty mountains that only the wild ones know

Valleys untouched by modern man, waters cold and deep

Hidden there among the pines, their secrets they still keep.

The forty-niners came and went in their endless search for gold

Some have never left here; their bones lie dead and cold

Little cabins they had built rotted; sagged and fell,

Places where they lived and died, the pines will never tell.

I've wandered in this wilderness,

and stopped and listened to the trees

Heard them tell their stories, as they chuckled in the breeze.

I've listened to the wild wolf sing his songs of woe

As he passed along the stories that he learned so long ago.

I've listened to the wilderness, heard the whispers in the pines

Seen the ghosts of travelers from some forgotten time

Their secrets, they have told me, are like footprints in the snow

Vanished in the morning light beneath the drifting snow.

35

Drums and Bugles

I hear the sound of distant drums, hear the bugles blow

This time I must sit and wait while sons and daughters go

They will go with heads held high, as others went before

I pray they will all return from this man's latest war

Yet some will die and others live, their bodies torn and battered

Some we will never see again; their ashes burnt and scattered.

If I could I'd take their place and shield them from the sight

The carnage of a battlefield when men and nations fight

Best would be no need for war; that all in peace could live,

The lion lie down with the lamb, this is the prayer I give.

Yet I am but a dreamer faced with reality,

I realize some must fight, if I wish to be free.

Space Travelers

They slipped the bonds of earth, lingered up on high

Sparkled in the heavens like a star up in the sky

Turning, they looked back on earth shining there below,

Green of forest, blue of sea and white of ice and snow

Is our world but a campsite glistening down below?

Are we bound for distant stars, only the heavens know.

Man is destined to strive, to try and touch a star

Most of us will never go but some will travel far,

Some of them may lose their lives and return to the sod

Grieve not when you hear their names, they died nearer God.

Again they will slip the chains of earth and blaze across the sky

They will sit and wait for others to hold man's banner high.

Beside You

As you wandered on life's highways, traveled far from home

Although you never knew it, you never walked alone

Remember when you first tried to walk, how hard it was to stand

I'm the one who helped you; you reached out and took my hand.

When you stood at the gates of Hell, I was right there by your side

I shed a joyous tear when you did not go inside.

No matter where you wander, if you need to walk or stand

I'll be there to help you, just reach out and take my hand

I will never judge you, but you will never walk alone

Call me when you're lost and tired and looking for a home.

Call me when you stumble or somehow lose your way

I've had lots of practice, finding those that went astray

When you walk your final mile, you will not walk alone

I'll be there beside you before the judgment throne.

Hold On

Remember that old Plymouth at the drive-in that first night

We cuddled close together, kissed and held on tight

In front of the church that day with you all dressed in white

Oh how your daddy cried, we kissed and held on tight

Then when our kids were born, in your eyes a special light

You smiled and passed them to me, we kissed and held on tight

Now my eyes are growing dimmer, let your face be my last sight

Darling, do not cry for me, kiss me and hold on tight.

Life's Load

This load is oh, so heavy, and the road ahead is long

I'm so lost and all alone, how can I travel on

The road ahead is icy, what if I should slip and fall

I have no one to help me, to aid me if I should call

How easy it would be to quit, lay down this heavy load

I need not the twists and turns I travel on this road.

Now a traveler stands beside me, with his own heavy load

He says; "I'll travel with you, we can help each other on the road,

Life's burdens can be lightened by others on the way,

Your own load can be lighter, if you help others on the way …

But there is one who will aid you,

lead you through the pain and strife,

He will always be there with you, as you travel through this life

He will always be there for you, no matter where you roam

His candle in the darkness will help to make it home

Then when you stand before the final judge

at the ending of your days,

Jesus will stand with you, if you helped others along the way."

The Lady of the Lake

Mist rises off the water, I see her standing there

Her gown as sheer as moonbeams, dewdrops in her hair

Eyes as blue as summer skies, hair like sun-kissed wheat

Without a word she disrobes, her gown lies at her feet

She seems to have an inner glow, her body so divine

Silently she blows me a kiss from lips as red as wine

She beckons me to join her; I reach out and take her hand

My heart racing wildly, we glide across the sand

Slowly we move into the water, feel its gentle, liquid caress

Now she turns to face me as my hands caress her breasts

Her arms reach out to hold me; our lips meet in a kiss

Tenderly, our bodies join in waves of gentle bliss

The warm and moonlit waters, the wavelets' gentle press

Heighten our arousal, magnify each sweet caress

I feel her body tremble, I hear her gentle sigh

Our bodies float together like stars across the sky

But this is only a dream, and she is gone as I awake

My gentle moonlit lover, the lady of the lake.

Again The Horsemen Ride

Their steeds paw at the earth, anticipation in their stride

The Horsemen are getting ready, again the four will ride

Pestilence, his armour black; disease coats him like slime

Silently he stands and waits, again will come his time.

Famine, like a skeleton; starvation is his game

Prepares once again to ride, fear follows his very name.

War, his armour red with blood; hones his thirsty sword

Nations tremble at his name, again he will cross the void.

Death towers over them; for he must take us all

Once again he prepares to ride, towards the bugles' call.

They have but to sit and wait; these horsemen out of time

Man once again calls them to feed from the darkness of our minds

Pestilence, Famine, War and Death; smoke rises where they stride

Again among the battle flags, the four again will ride.

The Game

When you play in the game of life,

you must take every hand they deal

You are not allowed to sit one out, no matter how you feel.

Take what you are given; throw your discards in the pile,

No matter what life deals you, face it with a smile.

One hand will yield four aces, the next hand just a knave

Throw away the poor cards, the good ones you can save.

You see, unlike a game of cards, in life you can hold back the best

Me, I kept the Queen of hearts; threw back all the rest.

The cards are shuffled endlessly, as we all play the game

One thing you can be sure of, no two hands are the same

A winner or a loser, what's the difference in a name

No matter, in the very end; except how you played the game.

The Compromise

The highway calls out to me, come take another run

Calls for me to take the road, head for the setting sun

That lonely endless blacktop somehow reaches deep inside

Touches something I can't name and once again I ride.

What is this deep inside me that causes me to roam?

Why can't I be like others, settle down and have a home?

A man touched with wanderlust, with diesel in my veins

To be happy I must move, no days can be the same

Yet even as I wander, I need to take a rest,

Like a swallow in the springtime, I return to her nest

She waits for me with open arms and welcomes me back home

Tied down by job and family, she has no need to roam.

Yet she too hears the highway as it calls and takes her man,

She fights it every way she knows and does the best she can.

That lonely empty highway, it keeps her family fed

Yet it also takes me away and keeps me from her bed,

Life becomes a compromise, as to work, I have to roam

She lives for when I can rest and spend some time at home.

Lonely Sounds

I have heard the lonely midnight train,

heard the lonesome Whippoorwill;

Listened to a sad Coyote as he cried atop a hill

I have heard the morning stillness shattered by a Loon

Heard a Wolf at midnight howling to the moon

These sounds can touch you, reach your heart and more

But no sound is as lonely as the slamming of a door.

Doors that slam in anger echo through your mind

A sound that will repeat itself across the sands of time.

Don't close a door in anger, don't slam down a phone

Both will echo in the silence when you find yourself alone.

Communication is the answer, take time out to hear

Silence is too lonely to carry through the years.

There Stands a Glass

There stands a glass, fill it up once again

Help me drown the memories and wash away the pain

The pain that comes from losing her and memories of better times

They run slowly thru my mind and are deadened by the wine.

Sitting on this bar stool I still can feel the pain

Help me drown those memories, fill that glass again

I can drown her memories in the warm glow of the wine

It helps to take the pain away so fill it one more time.

Why did she have to leave me, on this stool with all my pain

There stands a glass in front of me so fill it once again

There stands a glass, fill it up once again

I need to drown these memories and wash away my pain.

The Sentry

He stands upon a lonely hill upon some foreign shore

Dreams of home and family like those who went before

A sentry in the darkness watches thru the night

Protects those who rest behind him 'til the coming of the light

He could be a Roman Legionnaire or any soldier from the past

He stands on guard for others as he watches the night pass.

The Lady and Her Legacy

Her hands are cracked and callused

from the work that she has done

Her hair has lost its luster from the hours in the sun

She stands there in that faded dress she has had for oh, so long

Yet on her lips there is a smile, in her heart there is a song:

She's a woman and a mother, she's a lover and a wife

A very special person, the one who gave me life.

I've seen her when she was happy, and seen her when she was sad

Seen her cheer as I did well and cry when I was bad.

Would she be proud of what I am, the man that I've become

Would she even look at me and say that I was her son

She tried to teach me how to live and how to be a man

I'll try to make her proud of me and do the best I can.

Apart

She's weeping in the kitchen of her cold and lonely home

Final papers in her hand, he won't be coming home

He's out there on the highway with his anger and his pain

He got his copy yesterday, he won't go home again.

What drove her to another's arms, what caused him to go astray?

Was it something that they did or some things they did not say?

Were they ripped asunder or did they just drift apart?

Did they really tell each other what was within their hearts?

If each of them had listened to the other's doubts and fears

Would there be a need for all this pain, a need for all these tears

She's crying in the kitchen, he's on a highway all alone

Could a bit of talk have saved these two,

and stopped a broken home?

Did You

Did you tell her that you needed her,

when you held her in your arms,

Did you whisper softly to her, as you tried her many charms,

Did you talk about forever, as you took her to your bed,

Did the thought that she was married, just once go thru your head?

Back when you first met her, did you see her wedding band?

Just a simple band of gold, she wears upon her hand.

Now before I pull this trigger, there's one thing I'd like to know,

Did you ever think about me, and how I love her so?

Her cheating days are over, but yours are done as well

When they take me to the courtroom, my story I will tell,

The story of a broken heart, and about a cheating friend

When they put the noose around me, this story then will end.

Cold City

This city, dark and dangerous, streets cruel and cold

So many different stories waiting to be told

That hooker in the alley, what was it drove her there

Her life, pain and sorrow filled with dark despair

Drug dealers roam the street, marijuana, coke or hash

Anything is for sale if you have the cash

The business man bustles by, briefcase stuffed with paper

Thoughts of deals run thru his mind, consequences come later

A street vendor with his cart, tries to sell his wares

Traffic swirls around him, he neither sees or cares

A homeless person staggers by, shivers in the snow

I wonder what his story is or do I want to know

A cop stands on the corner, his face dead and cold

He's seen the worst this city has; no street is paved with gold

So many different stories waiting to be told

These streets so dark and dreary, stone hard and oh so cold.

I Go On

The road lies there ahead of me, a ribbon dark and still

Across a lonely valley and over a farther hill

This time I leave someone behind, I travel on alone

She's resting now; her body cold, beneath a lonely stone

Our farewells they've all been said, except within my mind

She will always travel with me; I'll not leave her behind.

She asked me not to grieve, just keep her memory dear

Here within my heart and mind it echoes oh so clear

Yet I must move on, she'd want that; this I know,

Yet she will travel with me, no matter where I go.

My pain will ease with time, my grief I know will pass

Memories of our happy times will stay with me and last

The road lies there ahead of me, a road of tar and stone

She will still travel with me, I do not go on alone.

The Moonbeam

A shy and gentle moonbeam quietly slipped into our room

Highlighted the one beside me as we lay there in the gloom

The moonbeam formed a halo around her pretty head

Her head upon my shoulder as we lay there in our bed.

Quietly I watched her in the light from up above

That gentle little moonbeam kissed the one I love

Quietly I lay there and watched her sleep and dream

Did I feel a gentle touch or was it just that stray moonbeam

She smiled and murmured quietly, but I heard her say my name

I knew then I was a winner; I had won big in life's game.

Big Rig Thunder

From Vancouver to Halifax and wherever they may roam

Millions of miles of highways that the big rigs call their home

Come stand beside that highway any time of night or day

Hear the mighty roll of thunder as they pass along their way

Across the snowcapped mountains and over hill and plain

No matter what the weather, be it sun or snow or rain

They travel any highway and haul any type of load

You know they would drive thru Hell if the Devil built a road.

Lights shine in the darkness, see the shine of chrome and steel

And a special breed of driver that sits behind the wheel

The rhythm of the engine and the whining of the tires

It sets their blood to pumping and sets their souls on fire

The highway is a special place, come listen to the song

The sound of rolling thunder as the big rigs move along

Come stand beside the highway any time of night or day

Hear the mighty roll of thunder as they pass along their way.

Darkness

She shivers in the darkness on this cold and lonely street

No money in her pocket and yet she needs to eat

Alone with just her memories in the darkness of the night

Just a shadow in the darkness underneath those neon lights

Many miles she's traveled from her family and her home

Now she cries here in the darkness, lost and all alone.

Traffic passes on the street as the city moves on by

Strange thoughts run through her mind, could it be her time to die

A semi rumbles down the street, lights and steel aglow

She stumbles down off the curb in the softly falling snow

Hear the screaming of the tires as the truck begins to slide,

The driver struggles with his rig, tries to control his ride

The truck shudders to a stop without an inch to spare

She huddles there on the street as people turn and stare.

Will her story have an end in this city dark and cold,

Life or death has no meaning here, just a story to be told…

Another Day

Darkness falls across the land, covers like a shroud

I move along the highway lost among the crowd

Shadows lose their sharpness as day turns into night

Commuters heading homeward in the softness of twilight

My rig comes up to speed as I work through the gears

I think back on all the roads I've traveled through the years.

North to lands of ice and snow, south down by the bay

The smoky smell of sagebrush, the scent of new-mown hay

East for a load of lobster, west for a load of grain

No matter what the season, be it sun or snow or rain

My lights shine through the darkness as I pass along the way

Another lonely driver, another load, another day.

Wanderers

Who are these ones who wander, that travel far from home

Spend their lives in travel on the highways all alone

What would they have been, another place, another time

Questions without answers tumble through my mind.

In the expansion to the west, did they drive the wagon train

As ever west they traveled over mountain, hill and plain,

Back when there were wooden ships crewed by iron men

Were they the ones that braved the sea

and brought them home again

Did they trek with Marco Polo across the Gobi, dry and wide,

Eyes searching ever onward, looking for the other side

Did they march with the Legion as they traveled far from home

Did they hold the Eagle high for the glory that was Rome

Where next will they wander, do their eyes lift to the sky

Perhaps to see a distant star, to travel, live or die,

For now, they have their big rigs and another heavy load,

They travel ever onward on that endless, open road.

Fallen Star

I stood upon a lonely hill and watched a falling star

It shone brightly in the heavens though I had seen it from afar

It streaked across the heavens from its home away up high

Tumbled down to meet the earth, to meet it and to die

So much like a mortal man and this brief life we live

As a star gives off its light so we must learn to give

It's only through others' eyes that our legacy lives on,

Else like a fallen star, we blaze and then are gone.

She

I hear her whisper softly, I hear her call my name

Once more she spreads her web, ensnares me once again

Again I run to her; fall 'neath her siren spell,

She takes me in and holds me, in an embrace I know so well,

Yet I know she lies to me, she holds many other men

Takes us in and uses us, then takes us back again.

My mistress is but a highway, who will kill me in the end

In some lonesome canyon, or around some deadly bend,

Still I hear her calling me as again she casts her spell,

I love her and I hate her, she knows me much too well.

Behind the Man

He tells me that he loves me, swears that he is mine

The vows we took together until the end of time

Now I sit in this empty room, tired and all alone

I wonder where he is tonight, as I wait for him to phone.

He will tell me that he misses me, and the places he has been

All the people he has met and all the sights he's seen

I'll tell him about our little girl, how she fell and skinned her knee

Cried out for her Daddy's arms, but had to come to me.

I'll tell him about our son, his home run at the game

How he ran the bases as the whole team called his name.

That big truck takes him places that we have never seen,

Even though he loves his family,

she's his damned old Highway Queen.

Many times I've wondered if he knows just how I feel,

It's hard to be the woman, behind the man behind the wheel.

Still I know I'm not alone, others know how I feel;

We're the ones who wait and worry, for the man behind the wheel.

Silent Wonder

Mist rises softly from the lake, I hear a wild loon cry

Its call echoes thru the pines that reach and touch the sky

The gentle whisper of the wind sighs in the silent night

The heavens shine in splendor with the twinkle of starlight

I stand in silent wonder and take in all I can

The magnificence of nature and the insignificance of man.

I Held His Hand

I saw the big rig start to slide, as he started down the hill,

I saw the trailer jackknife and I saw the whole load spill;

I saw the impact with the guardrail, then the rocks and trees below

I started down to help him, but I knew I was too slow.

A mangled pile of twisted steel, glass shattered all around,

I knelt down and took his hand, as he lay there on the ground.

I covered him with my jacket, to shield him from the rain,

I heard him whisper softly, and I heard him say her name;

Tell my wife I love her, and tell my children not to cry,

Then he gave a little smile, and then the trucker died.

They found us there together; I could not leave his side,

Though I never knew his name; I held his hand and cried.

Sinner Man

Yes, I have led a sinful life, but I will pay the price;

Just once, God, let me look upon the face of Jesus Christ,

Please let me touch the hand that bled at Calvary

Though they nailed Him to the cross, He set the whole world free.

Once, let me look upon the man that walked on the water

Then I will face the fires of Hell,

though the Devil makes them hotter.

What's that? I have no need to go; I may stay here by the throne,

You say my love for your son, has made for me a home?

My sins have been forgiven; my soul has been set free,

Jesus lives for everyone, but He also died for me.

Fire on the Mountain

Fire on the mountain; flames reach for the sky

Among the smoke and cinders, dreams and hopes have died.

Homes destroyed in moments as a wall of flame goes by

Memories and hopes and dreams are ashes in the sky.

A forest turned to cinders, smoke shrouds the sun and moon,

The sky takes on an eerie glow, darkness falls at noon.

Water bombers drop their loads on a scene from Dante's Hell

Firefighters take a stand, yet still the monster swells.

Fire on the mountain, flames reach for the sky

Below them in the valley is a town that will not die.

They will lose some houses; those they can build again

This town now works together, thru its troubles and its pain

Fire on the mountain, people pray and cry

They will all fight together, their town it will not die.

Last Gunfighter

He stumbles from the barroom out to the hot, high noonday sun

His right hand like a talon, on his right hip rides a gun

He was once the fastest gun alive; he may be the fastest still

The notches on his pistol mark the many men he killed

Last of a dying breed, the gunfighters of the west

Time and age has taken its toll and killed off all the rest

But he thought someone had called him out,

so he stumbled to the street

Somewhere in the heat and haze is the one that he must beat

He steps down off the sidewalk, and thru the haze he sees a glow

He reaches for his deadly gun but this time he is too slow.

Struck down by a pickup truck, he lies there in the street

The last man of a lonely breed died with his boots upon his feet.

Daydreams

She wanders softly thru my mind like smoke from a candle flame

Her hand reaches out to me and I hear her call my name

Her lips, so warm and tender, her breath as sweet as wine

I hear her footsteps by my side, they echo thru my mind

Her hand reaches out to me, gentle as the falling snow

Our bodies and our souls unite in a dance that lovers know

Then I awake to reality, two thousand miles from home

A sailor on a concrete sea, adrift and all alone

The highway rolls beneath my wheels;

I hear those big wheels whine

Again she reaches out to me, a daydream in my mind.

A Voice

A voice came on my CB just the other night

Even though he knew my name I knew this was not right

He knew all the people I had hurt and even knew their names,

He knew about the things I'd done where others took the blame.

He said that he was waiting until it was my time to go,

He said he had a place for me in the fires down below.

I tried to change the channel, but he was on every one

There was no place for me to hide, nowhere for me to run.

Then I heard another voice, that seemed to come from all around

A voice that was so sweet and clear, my heart melted at the sound.

It offered me salvation if I would but change my life.

It offered me eternal peace and an ending to all strife.

Tears came to my tired eyes as I pulled off to the side

Silently I said a prayer, and offered him a ride

He said I could stay with him, since I had made the choice,

Surrounded by the love and hope that I heard in his voice

Forgiven by the Son of God, my soul has been set free

Now I travel down life's highway, Jesus Christ and me.

The Old Man

His hair had turned snowy white and his face was lined and old

His back was bent and crooked from working in the cold,

Both bow-legged and pigeon-toed from the saddles he had filled

His eyes still held a steely glint that showed he'd seen his fill

His smile was bright and sunny, and his voice was deep and clear

He told us all about his life and the things that he held dear,

He told us about a cattle drive in the spring of eighty-five

Told us about the cowboys, and they seemed to come alive.

He told us all about the war they had fought, so far from home

The men that fought beside him, not all had made it home

He told us of a lady he had wooed and then had won

Told us about his children, two daughters and a son.

Ho spoke of a nation, from sea to shining sea

He spoke of the men that died to keep that nation free.

He said there is a reason these stories I have told,

This nation now is yours to keep, as I am growing old

Liberty, truth and justice with courage as a glue

This, along with trust in God, is what will see you thru.

The Old Man
Part 2

Now I too, am growing old and my hair is turning gray,

Will youth listen to my story; hear what I have to say

The banner now I pass to you, you daughters and you sons,

Make vigilance your watchword and the battle will be won.

Remember too, your history and the leaders of the past,

This heritage of freedom is something that must last.

Her Eyes

Eyes that show a flash of green if she thinks I have been bad

Eyes that can melt the coldest heart if she is feeling sad

Softness within those eyes when she sees a little child

Fire flashes from those eyes when she gets a little wild

I've seen those eyes look tired and old at the ending of a day

Yet come alive with passion if she thinks it's time to play

I've seen those eyes filled with tears from sorrow and from pain

I have seen them light like a summer sky as it clears after a rain

Those eyes so ever-changing and all the things they see,

There are times I wonder, what do they see in me?

Autumn Pause

The leaves have turned to red and gold;

night brings a touch of frost

Blackbirds swirl across the sky, like they may be lost,

In the autumn valleys, elk bugle for a mate

A whitetail prances across the draw and waters by the lake.

Salmon brave the rapids, to spawn and then to die

In the distance hear the wild goose call, see their V across the sky

The busy little squirrel hides his winter's feed

Grasses cure upon the stem, winds scatters autumn's seed

A season of transition, of death and yet rebirth

Soon the snows will come to cover Mother Earth

I pause in my journey and rest along the way

Autumn is my season now, as I too am turning gray.

Two Lovers

Dark was the color of the night in the dungeon where he lay,

They will hang him in the morning in the harsh light of the day.

No more along the high road, sword and pistol by his side

No more; "Stand and deliver;" no longer will he ride.

Then, a light, outside his cell, the turning of a key

There stands the jailer's daughter, come to set him free.

A horse tied behind the jail, a ship waits at the quay

Two lovers board holding hands and the ship slowly slips away.

The hangman's noose hangs empty, a cell door swings open wide

Two lovers cling together as they set sail upon the tide.

Three Prayers

In a quiet suburban home near the closing of the day

A woman pauses from her chores and takes the time to pray

She prays for her husband, in his big rig all alone,

She prays for her eldest son, in the service, far from home.

Amid the bustle of a truck stop, somewhere along the way,

A driver does his logbook and takes some time to pray

He prays for his wife at home, waiting by the phone

He prays for the son he raised,

now in some country far from home.

A foxhole dug in foreign soil beneath a setting sun

A soldier says a quiet prayer as he reaches for his gun

His prayer is for his Mother, who waits for him at home,

His prayer is for his Father, in his big rig all alone.

This family bound by love and faith will withstand any strife

They know that thru the power of prayer they are given eternal life.

Dragon Tales

The Knight slew the Dragon and rescued the Lady Fair

Then they rode off to the castle, her with flowers in her hair

That was in a fairy tale; real life is not the same

The dragons that I have to face don't want to be slain.

Mortgages and payments that last for years and years

Taxed by the government right up to my ears

One kid needs new braces, the other needs new shoes

Every time that I call home I just get more bad news.

Where oh where is my magic sword, where is my prancing steed

Where is my magic armor in this, my time of need,

Merlin, wave your magic wand, make my dragons go away

Give me a little time to rest; let me and my Lady play

Still I know I will stagger on, I'll fight until the end,

Slaying Dragons one by one, until my story ends.

Errant Knight

Like a warrior from some forgotten past he travels across the land

His shiny steed of steel and glass answers to his command

Across the land from sea to sea, the highway is his home

North and south, east and west, always he must roam.

His engine sings of freedom, love of an open road

His tires tell of lonely miles beneath a heavy load

His headlights burning brightly turn dark night into day

The thunder of his passage echoes across the way.

A hero from our forgotten past, or just another man

A driver on the long highway who does the best he can

Surrounded by humanity yet still he stands alone

An errant Knight on a steed of steel, the highway is his home.

What will you remember

What will you remember when it's time for me to go

Will you remember how I held you and how I loved you so;

Maybe you'll remember me being on the road

You slept in our bed alone, my side was oh, so cold,

Will you remember what I whispered, as I held you oh, so tight

Will you just remember the long and lonely nights?

Will you remember how we kissed on the day that we were wed

Or just the nights you spent alone in our marriage bed,

Will you remember how I looked the day you took my ring

Or just that you were alone as I worked for everything.

Don't remember me as a driver, remember me as a man

Remember me as a husband who does the best he can

Remember me as a lover who walked with you stride for stride

Remember me as the man that took you for his bride

Remember all the good times as I will remember you,

Remember, Darling, most of all, I gave my heart to you.

The Light

Now I hear the screen door slam and hear your old car start

Again I hear the words we said that tore our world apart

I walk across the silent room and pick your ring up off the floor,

Your words echo through my mind, "I don't love you anymore."

This home once filled with light and love

now feels so dark and cold,

I think of all our dreams and plans, now crushed or placed on hold.

Then through my tears I hear a sound, I turn and see your face

Our salty tears co-mingle as our arms embrace.

I hear you say, "I love you," I slip your ring back on your hand,

It's surprising how much light is shed by just this little band.

Our problems are not over, but we will make things right

With a little help from God above and His eternal light.

The Waitress

She smiles and pours your coffee, asks what you would like to eat

She is trying to be cheerful while she is dying on her feet

She's worried about her child at home, and the cough he had today

She's putting in too many hours for just too little pay.

She laughs at your little jokes as she sweeps up the floor

She even smiles as you make a pass, but she's heard this all before.

She's mostly working for the tips and living day-to-day,

She dreams about the life she would have if she struck it rich today

She's a traveler on life's highway, who walks many weary miles

She brightens up so many lives with just her little smiles.

Greasy Grass Revisited

Again I walk this prairie land, what draws me to this place

Again I feel the restless wind blow cold upon my face,

Once more I hear the battle sounds, echoes come from all around

The thunder of the horse's hooves seems to shake the ground

Now I hear a rifle speak, I stumble and I fall

My flesh is torn asunder by the rifle's deadly ball

I feel the dusty, short grass as I struggle to arise

I hear the rifle speak again and a veil comes to my eyes

No more will I race the wind or watch an Eagle fly

I struggle for another breath; I do not wish to die

Again I feel the prairie wind as I kneel upon this ground

I feel the tears run down my face and fall on hallowed ground

What gives me this connection to this battle long ago

I stop and say a silent prayer, rise and turn to go

I see them all before me, men both white and red

To me they seem to whisper, to you we are not dead

The earth may hold our bodies, yet still our souls are free,

A reminder of the cost of war for those with eyes to see.

Tired Eyes

His eyes tell his story, the endless open road

Too many miles behind him, too many heavy loads

He has faced prairie dust and roads of snow and ice

Days of glaring sunshine, he has paid the price

Like roads upon a map, run the lines upon his face

He remembers those he left behind

as he moved from place to place.

There were those who cared for him, he tried but loved and lost

Now he keeps on moving, no matter what the cost.

The highway has become his life, his truck it is his home,

Onward ever onward, forever he will roam

His eyes tell the story, a tired and lonely man,

Living his life day by day and getting by the best he can.

The Forgotten

Deep in the concrete jungle the streets are cold and mean,

Back in a dirty alley where they will not be seen

Far away from prying eyes, the forgotten and the lost

They struggle just to survive, no matter what the cost.

Food comes from a dumpster, shoes from the Sally Ann,

Shelter is a cardboard box beside a garbage can.

Who are these forgotten people in this living hell

What brings them to this place, what stories will they tell

A young girl from a broken home, who suffered from abuse

A man who lost his wife and home to hard drugs and to booze

So many different stories; yet they all end the same,

Hidden from our mundane lives, in an alley with no name.

Silence

Silence all around me, I miss the sound of birds;

People's mouths are moving, but I do not hear the words.

Thirty years of driving, listening to the tires whine

I miss the sounds of silence, like the wind among the pines.

The roaring of the diesel as the miles went rushing by,

Has stolen away the chance to hear a baby cry.

Silence falls around me, I feel lost and all alone;

I cannot understand you when I call you on the phone.

The harder that I listen, the less I hear the words,

The diesel took your voice from me, and God, I miss the birds.

A Flower

Taillights string out in front of me like beads upon a chain

Headlights lose their brightness in the slowly falling rain

The wipers beat a rhythm keeping perfect time

The lanes stretch out before me marked by the dotted line

There beside the highway a flower struggles to survive

A lonely flash of color in the grayness of my drive

The gray of the season broken by a touch of green

Winter struggles to hold on, spring struggles to be seen

Another season passes like a footstep out of time

Marked only by a daffodil by a lonely highway sign.

Gentle Passage

A cabin window glistens with the soft glow of candlelight

An old man sits in silence throughout the quiet night

A fireplace, a book and a simple glass of wine

In the flickering firelight, memories from out of time

His smile is soft and gentle as he looks into the flame

Faces dance in the fire and seem to call his name

One face stands out from all the rest, one that he held dear

He seems to hear her voice again so soft, so sweet, so clear.

The book falls from his hand and tumbles to the floor,

The old man breathes a gentle sigh and then he breathes no more

Somewhere in the distance a lonely church bell rings,

There above the cabin, could that be Angel wings?

Eternal Drive

Drive with me to the edge of time; let's see what awaits us there

Fly with me to the Milky Way; I'll place stardust in your hair

Journey back with me to Jerusalem; at the time of Jesus' birth

Park with me in The Sea of Tranquility;

we'll watch the sunrise o'er the Earth

Walk with me in a peaceful land; where the lion lies with the lamb

Wade with me in the stream of life; come closer and take my hand

Dance with me in that special dance; that only lovers know

Stay with me until eternity; then I'll let you go.

Broken Heart

I gave you a little ring; you gave me one too

A promise until the end of time that we would both be true

That vow I held so solemn you have seen fit to break

Now you are in another's arms. Did I make some mistake?

Was it something I have done that sent you to another

Did you find me wanting as a man, or as a lover?

While I was on the road, did you spend too much time alone,

I tried to make it up to you when I called you on the phone.

I guess you have your reasons, so I must set you free

If you ever change your mind, then come back home to me

Perhaps my broken heart will mend, and I can love again,

Can I ever learn to trust after all this pain?

Listen

I have listened to the whispering wind

and heard the northern lights

Heard the chuckle of a stream and heard a campfire speak at night

I listened to the tales they told of times so long ago,

Tales of summer sunshine and the blowing, drifting snow

Of a cowboy from El Paso, down by the Rio Grande

Tales of how he lived and loved and died there in the sand.

Tales about a ghostly ship forever doomed to wander,

Stories of a man they knew who walked upon the water.

Tales of the 49'ers and their search for gold and fame

Of a man that they called Blackbeard who sailed the Spanish Main

They told me of many men, black, yellow, red and white,

I've listened to them whisper around me in the night.

I've heard their stories of land and air and sea,

I wonder in the future, will they also speak of me.

I hope they might speak well of me, and make my exploits glisten,

The very least they can say, is that when they spoke, I listened.

Our Lady

A child of many parents who struggled to survive

She fought for her independence to prove she was alive

Young, rash and full of fire, now that she was free

She spread her wings and stretched herself from sea to shining sea

She had her problems as brother fought with brother

Blue and gray they fought and died at the hands of one another

Her sons fought on foreign soils to help hold back the night

They fought and died as free men to defend that which is right

From Europe to Korea her sons and daughters gave their all

Even in the haze of Vietnam they answered freedom's call

Grown now into a lady, but tempered hard as steel

She stands for truth and freedom, bends but does not kneel

Blindsided by a sucker punch from those she has fought to save

Many of her sons and daughters sent to an early grave

Shaken to her very core from the ashes she does rise

A pause to mourn her fallen, then fire flashes in her eyes

The innocent will know mercy but the guilty they will pay

Those who have riled our lady shall live to rue the day.

She Cries

He's ready to leave again and she gives a little sigh

She waves as he drives away, then she has a little cry

He will phone home later and she'll be waiting for the call,

After she hears from him, another tear will fall.

She will tuck the children in, at the ending of the day

She will stop and think of him, and as she cries she'll pray

She prays to keep him safe from harm

and to bring him safely home,

She cries because she misses him and feels so all alone.

Still, she has some friends to call, to help her do what is right

Still, she sheds a little tear, in the long and lonely night.

Gentle Memories

The quiet dusty gravel road, the scent of new-mown hay

Takes me back in memory to dreams of yesterday

The evening song of the whippoorwill, so lonesome he could cry

The softness of the summer grass, where my love and I did lie

Grain fields blowing in the wind, corn all in their rows

The scent of many growing things as gentle breezes blow

The freshness of the open land after a summer rain

In my mind I wander back to my youth again

These memories I cherish of a slower, gentler time

Vanished now into the past, but still held in my mind.

Empty Arms

The rhythm of the highway seduces with her charms

Yet still I reach out, to hold you in my arms

In my mind you whisper, and I hold you, oh, so tight

Gently our bodies merge together in the night,

Yet I awake with empty arms and an aching in my heart,

So lonely are the nights when we are apart.

The highway winds and wanders, calls for me to roam

Still I reach with empty arms, for what I left at home,

Along beside the highway, a trail of broken hearts,

A reminder of the many lives this highway tore apart.

Summer Storm

The darkness of a sullen sky is split by a sword of light

The deep harsh roll of thunder echoes thru the night

Raindrops touch the dusty soil as the wind begins to rise

Thunder chases lightning across the darkened sky

Winds swirl across the land as bushes dance and sway

Rain soaks the thirsty soil as the storm moves along the way

Washed by Mother Nature's hand the grass and trees are green

The air takes on a fresher scent and the entire world seems clean.

Dreams and Wishes

Wishes simply are the dreams we have while we are awake

Dreams are only other trails that we yearn to take

Dreams can take us to a world that no one has ever seen

Make a man into a pirate king or a woman into a queen

Turn a car into a rocket ship that will cruise among the stars

A trip to the corner store ends on Jupiter or Mars

A trip into the future or back to a vanished past

Yet our dreams are fleeting and are not meant to last

Yet dreams can also be a seed, which planted, can then grow

If we strive to live our dreams, how far can mankind go?

A Woman's Power

What is this gentle power that a woman has over a man

Is this something natural, just part of nature's plan?

We met; I like a fledgling that had never walked, or ran

I trembled as we met and then she touched my hand

My heart learned how to sing when I first touched her lips

Sweeter than a honeycomb from where the honey drips

Later in the pale moonlight she taught me how to fly

Gently as we joined in love my spirit touched the sky

I soared aloft on golden wings and joined with her in flight

Lifted by a woman's love I touched the stars that night

A woman's gentle power, this thing that we call love

Sent by our creator from somewhere up above.

Afterglow

Hear the lonely whippoorwill echo thru the misty light

Evening shadows lengthen as day passes into night

A pale moon softly glistens in the gentle summer sky

Casts his light upon a meadow wherein two lovers lie

Daisies bow their pretty heads and shyly turn away

A night breeze softy whisper to the grasses where they lay

Wrapped in each other's arms, passions ebb and flow

Two bodies in the pale moonlight, dance in the afterglow.

Time will Tell

We know not what awaits us, maybe heaven, maybe hell;

Whatever is ahead of us, only time will tell

We are on a journey with many roads to choose

Take one, you are a winner; take another and you lose.

I've been down a winding road and touched the gates of hell,

I have heard the stories other travelers had to tell

Tales of woes and troubles better left untold

Dreams of a better life with riches and with gold,

Yet I march to my own drum, so proud to be a man

Tempered by the fires, I'll do the best I can.

When I stand before that final judge I'll hold my head up high

Take my judgment like a man and look him in the eye,

Maybe heaven, maybe hell, he knows where I will rest

He also knows how hard I tried and gave this trip my best.

I've tried to walk the narrow path, but many times I strayed

I just hope he remembers those I helped along the way.

I know not what awaits me, maybe heaven, maybe hell

Still I know I've done my best; now only time will tell.

Somebody's Knocking

Somebody's knocking; oh, Angel, please let me in

You say I'm the Devil, but our love is no sin

You knew about me but you never dreamed

I'd wear cowboy boots and faded old jeans.

You know we can have one hell of a night

I'll hold you close in the misty moonlight

You know I love you, Angel, please let me in

Your Devil is calling and our love is no sin

My love is a fire, can you feel the heat

My temperature's rising, can you feel my heartbeat

Come with me, my Angel, let me teach you to fly

Our love, it will take us to the mountains so high

You say I'm the Devil, but our love is no sin

Somebody is knocking, darling, please let me in.

The Meadow

Walk with me to a meadow where the summer wind blows free

Rest in the grass of the meadow in the shade of a tall oak tree

Bathe with me in its quiet stream, its waters fresh and clear

Let us dry 'neath the summer sun and let our worries disappear

Dance with me in the meadow in the gentle cool moonlight

Hold hands as we walk thru the meadow,

watch the falling of the night

Lie with me in the meadow; let my shoulder be your pillow

Stay forever and a day; make a home with me in the meadow.

A Child's Cry

Somewhere a line is written, somewhere a tear will fall

Somewhere a child is born, somewhere a star will fall

One man will live while another dies, another doesn't care

A mother rocks a tiny child and weeps in quiet despair

A man stumbles thru the night awash in drugs and pain

A woman waits at home for love and knows she waits in vain

A child cries into the night lost and all alone

A child is born into a life inside a broken home

Somewhere a line is written and again a tear will fall

A child lives, a child cries and no one cares at all.

Helping Hand

Has someone ever helped you out, maybe smoothed your way

Perhaps just some little thing that helped you thru your day,

Could someone have taken your place, so you could have a rest

Maybe they just urged you on, so you could do your best.

Maybe just a shoulder to cry on in the night

Perhaps just a guiding hand that led you to the light

Sometimes help is subtle and hard for us to see

Sometimes it stands tall and proud like a mountain or a tree.

Perhaps someone helped you out, and you never took the time

To thank them or to pay them back, somewhere down the line.

Don't worry much about it, as they didn't work for pay

Just pass along that helping hand somewhere along the way

Neighbors helping neighbors is how strangers become friends

That's how we keep in balance, from the beginning to the end

Stop to help someone, wave and then be gone

Don't ask for pay or gratitude, just smile and pass it on.

Dark City Night

Darkness falls across the land as day turns into night
City that never sleeps glows with electric light

Cloaked now in the darkness on streets dark and mean
People hidden from the light prepare to take the scene

A mugger in the alley at 36th and Grand
Blood shines wetly on the knife he holds in his hand

A hooker on the corner of 21st and Forestlawn
Trembles from her latest fix as she looks for a John

An old drunk in the alley between Oak and Vine
Huddles in his cardboard house and slowly drinks his wine

A homeless man is diving behind Galloway Meats
Searching thru the garbage to find something to eat

A cop car turns the corner and slowly drives on by
You can see he has seen it all by the hardness in his eyes

Some college kids are searching as they drive on past
The druggie on the corner sells them a bag of grass

A semi slowly rumbles by, sidelights burning bright
The mall in the next block gets its deliveries at night

Night in the concrete jungle has both predator and prey
Hidden in the darkness far from the light of day.

Still Working

I know I'm not what you wanted,

not the White Knight of your dreams,

I never had any armor, just these old faded jeans

My ride is a big truck, not a steed of purest white

I've never even seen a lance or held a sword of light.

I'm not into slaying dragons, but I think I've known a few,

The best part of my life so far has been in meeting you.

Well, I did a little checking with my maker and you see,

He says He is still working; He's just not done with me.

I'm still a work in progress, so if you can wait a bit

You yet might get your wishes before He has to quit.

I won't make any promises, but if you have some time

There's no telling what you could find somewhere down the line.

A Picture

I hold a vision in my mind that lingers with me yet

A vision of a lady on the very night we met

Dark brown hair and ruby lips and eyes that shone so bright

I tried not to let it show how she stole my heart that night

Who would have ever guessed way back in the past

How long I'd see that vision and how long my love would last

The years slipped by so quickly I never saw them go

The time has come to throttle back and set the speed to slow

Let's walk down to the river like we did in times gone past

Take along a blanket and spread it on the grass

Just sit there on our blanket together hand in hand

Watch the clouds make shadows as they pass across the land

Yes, the years have changed us and now we are growing gray

Yet still I see the vision of the lady that I met that happy day.

The Lady Cries

Alone with Lady Liberty in the harbor where she stands

I swear I saw her crying, saw her tears fall to the sands

One tear she shed for liberty, many died that she be free

Their names are written in the stars for the entire world to see.

Another tear was shed for truth, that none should need to lie

A concept that's as old as time for which our sons have died

A tear was shed for justice, equality shown to one and all

The scales must wear a blindfold or else our nation falls.

For the victims of disaster another teardrop lands

They were falling all around me, alone there in the sand

Could I be the only one that shares her doubts and fears?

Could I be the only one that sees our Lady's tears?

Now others crowd around me, I do not stand alone

Together we will dry her tears and protect our Lady's home.

A Common Soldier

Sword to sword at Thermopolis where our blood ran in the sand

We stood before the Eagle in Rome and other lands

Marched against Napoleon at a place called Waterloo

Stood with Washington at the Delaware and with the gray and blue

Fought in the muddy trenches of the Somme and at Dunkirk's
bloody sands

Froze and fought at the Chosen Reservoir and in many other lands

We have won a million battles and lost a million more

Our bones lie pale and broken on mountains and by shore

I am nothing but a common soldier but I do not fight for gold

I fight for home and family and will not be bought or sold

I have seen the face of evil and against it I will stand

I will always fight for freedom in this or other lands

Others will come to take my place if by chance I fall

Freedom, home and family calls out to one and all.

Our Trail

We have walked this trail together for oh so many years

A trail made sunny by our smiles or watered by our tears

Sometimes the trail would wind but we never lost our way

Sometimes the trail was rocky but we took it day by day

Looking back I see some things perhaps we should have changed

Still if I had a chance I'd walk that trail again

Yes I might miss a couple curves, maybe straighten out a few

The only thing I wouldn't change – I'd walk again with you.

Endless Sky

Up high above the asphalt we wander across the land

From sea to shining sea over mountains, fields and sand

Our big old diesels thunder, we hear the tires cry

We travel ever onward beneath an endless sky

Night falls all around us, taillights shine so bright

Like a row of beads upon a string we thunder thru the night.

Ever on we wander as daylight follows night

Onward, ever onward, headlights shining bright

This load goes to Texas; the next one goes to Maine

Then north across to Winnipeg, then do it all again

Ever doomed to wander beneath an endless sky

Steel ships upon a concrete sea, the diesels thunder by.

An Old Truck

Out back in the wrecking yard covered by a ton of dust

A veteran of the highway sits and slowly turns to rust

No headlights now to show the way,

her windshield cracked and glazed

Does she sit and ponder what she has seen in better days?

Trips across the prairie lands, beneath an endless sky

Her diesel singing loud and strong as the miles went rushing by

Memories of a winter mountain pass, choked with ice and snow

She traveled over highways where Angels feared to go.

North along the ice roads, south to sand and sun

East to west, then back again, oh, how she loved to run

Does she think about the people that slept upon her bed

Does she remember all they did and all the things they said?

Now she's back there in the corner and the days slip slowly by

LOOK – there upon her windshield, could a big truck really cry?

A Simple Life

A quiet little country church on a gentle summer morn

Bells ring in celebration as a little girl is born

All the people in the chapel pray for guidance from above

May this child receive the blessing of God's eternal love.

Twenty years thereafter dressed in a gown of white

Bells ring out in celebration, as the woman becomes a wife

All the people in the chapel pray for guidance from above

May God smile upon this union and give them eternal love.

Sixty years later, now just one lonely church bell rings

As a soul ascends to Heaven guided by an Angel's wings

All the people in the chapel pray for guidance from above

A prayer for their salvation and for God's eternal love.

Let's Stop

Let's all stop and take a break, take a look around

Despite all our problems, we stand on solid ground

Lands of peace and plenty, from sea to shining sea

Where our forefathers fought and died to keep us proud and free

Two nations like no others, our border just a line

Sons of a common mother, brothers for all time

North to lands of constant snow, south to sun and sand

I've seen so many wonders as I travel across this land

Cattle by the thousands, fields of wheat and corn

Rivers, lakes and forests where the wild ones still are born

Majestic snowcapped mountains, wild and rugged shores

Farm lands oh so fertile, we need not ask for more

Stop and take a look around, thank God for what you see

Two nations proud and friendly, two peoples proud and free.

Atlantic Shore

The rocky eastern coastline, the Atlantic, cold and dark

Forests of oak and maple, winter limbs so bare and stark,

Birch with a shine of white, pine trees green and deep,

What lies beneath their shadows, what secrets do they keep.

Tales of ship-wrecked sailors who rested for a day,

Watching for a rescue ship to anchor in the bay,

Perhaps an Indian hunter, who rested from the chase,

Watching, ever-vigilant, on guard here in this place.

Could there be a Viking rune, carved deep within a stone

Did they live or did they die in this forest all alone

A lonely, quiet shoreline lashed by wind and sea,

How many stories will it tell to those with eyes to see.

Winding Road

A highway stretches out ahead, a ribbon dark and cold

Who knows what lies ahead of me and what the future holds

There are hills that I must climb, junctions I must take

Curves I must negotiate and decisions I must make.

Narrow bridges I must cross, icy roads where I may slip

So many dangers lie in wait as I travel on my trip

I meet with many others as I travel on my way

Some of them will aid me; some will try to make me stray,

Which way I go is up to me, the decision mine alone

A little luck and trust in God, and I will make it home.

My Luck

If it wasn't for my bad luck, I wouldn't have any luck at all

Every time that I stand up, I seem to trip and fall

Between troubles that I have at home, and trouble on the road

Many times I stop to wonder, how can I pull this load.

One child is in the hospital; the truck has broken down,

The parts will have to be shipped in, from some other town.

Doctors, lawyers and mechanics, all folks that I must pay

Each one has their hand out, just can't wait another day.

Still I struggle onward, too dumb and scared to stop

Always on the bottom, striving for the top.

Sit with me

Sit with me for a moment, and watch the clouds drift by

See the patterns that they make as they drift across the sky

Watch them ever-changing as they move with wind and time

Let them draw a picture upon the surface of your mind.

Remember that the cloud you see, drifting by today,

The same cloud the Romans saw, from the hilltops of their day.

Nations will rise and nations will fall, now, as in the past,

Simple things like clouds and earth are the only things that last.

Sit with me for a moment like others from the past

There is no need for word or deed; it's the simple things that last.

A Simple Hand

How is it that a simple hand can say so very much

A mother quiets a little child, simply with a touch.

Friendship and all it means, conveyed with a firm shake

Sorrow for another's loss, a touch is all it takes.

A hearty pat upon the back, for a job that was well done,

A friendly punch upon the arm, for a race that was well run.

The gentle touch of a friend says that they understand

Dogs and cats feel the love pour from their master's hand.

A lover says a million words with just a soft caress

And yet it is a child's touch that I remember best.

Holding on to just one finger, as they learn to walk and stand

A child gives their trust and love with just their tiny hand.

A Trucker's Prayer

Oh, Lord, bless all those truckers out there on the roads,

Help them and protect them as they haul their loads,

Watch over them by day and night,

Keep them always in your sight,

Give their tires some extra grip,

So they will neither slide nor slip.

Keep them alert both night and day,

As they travel on their way,

Then when they lie in their lonely beds,

Place thoughts of home within their heads.

After their run, please bring them home,

So they will know they are not alone,

Bless all those truckers on the roads,

Protect them as they haul their loads.

When their lives are over, and they stand before your throne,

Let the final log book entry be – the trucker has gone home.

Children

A baby, so like an angel, asleep in the cradle of your arms

Protected by your strength and love, sheltered from all harm

A child so like a kitten, tumbles across the floor

Full of life and energy and mischief by the score

A youngster so like a puppy, born to leap and run

Eyes searching the horizon, looking for some fun

Teens so like a colt on ice, not knowing where to turn

Slip and slide on dangerous ground but with energy to burn

Children never holding still but not knowing where to start.

Today they make you laugh, but tomorrow they break your heart

The leaders of tomorrow with goals that they must keep

Trouble in the daytime, but angels while they sleep.

The Old Truck

How very many lonely miles passed beneath her wheels,

Does she dream of passing lanes, this hulk of rusted steel?

Out behind a breaker's shed, with others of her kind

Does she miss the high road, the rhythm and the whine?

If only she could talk, what stories she would tell

The many drivers she has known and the roads she knew so well.

The many loads she carried, and the places she has been,

Does she dream of former days, this sad old highway queen?

Gently we load her on a deck, and then I tie her down

She's going to be recycled; they are going to melt her down,

Perhaps she will rise again and know her former glory,

Perhaps this was but chapter one, and not the final story.

Printed in the United States
72377LV00002B/40-138